The Everyth

The Medite

A Quickstart Guide To Weight Loss Solution With Meal Plan And Recipes To Reset Your Body, And Boost Your Energy! Tailor Made Meal Plan Plus Quick And Delicious Recipes, Tips To Eat Healthy And Lose Weight Eating

Written By

HOLLIE MCCARTHY, RDN

Table of Contents

INTRODUCTION

Thank you for purchasing this book!

Following the Mediterranean diet means ensuring a balanced intake of various macronutrients (carbohydrates, proteins, and lipids or fats), so distributed:

- 45-60% carbohydrates, mainly complex (such as cereal starches)
- 10-12% proteins
- 20-35% fats with a percentage of saturated fats (present in almost all animal products except fish) of less than 10%.

More in detail, this dietary pattern guarantees our organism:

- **proteins in moderate quantity and mainly from the vegetable origin;**
- **carbohydrates with low index and glycemic load**, with **simple sugars almost absent;**
- high ratio of monounsaturated/saturated fatty acids;
- antioxidant substances (beta-carotene, tocopherols, vitamins C and E, polyphenols) in large quantities;
- **an abundance of calcium, magnesium, and potassium, low amounts of sodium.**

Enjoy your reading!

BREAKFAST

Cinnamon sugar donut muffins

SERVES: 12

INGREDIENTS

- Donut Muffins
- 1 1/2 cups Almond Flour
- 1/2 cup Erythritol, powdered
- 2 tbsp. Psyllium Husk Powder
- 1/2 cup Heavy Cream
- 1/3 cup Salted Butter
- 2 large Eggs
- 1 1/2 tsp. Baking Powder and 1/2 tsp. Orange Extract
- 1/4 tsp. Nutmeg and 1/4 tsp. Allspice and 1/4 tsp. Liquid Stevia
- 1/8 tsp. Ground Clove and 1/8 tsp. Ground Ginger
- Cinnamon "Sugar" Coating

DIRECTIONS

1. Start by putting 1/3 cup butter into a small pan over medium-low heat. You want to let this melt and stir occasionally as you get the other ingredients ready.

2. In a spice grinder, add 1/2 cup erythritol and 1 twig of clove (if you're using pre-ground clove, skip the twig). We're going to grind these together to save a bit of time.

3. Add all dry ingredients to a bowl. 1 1/2 cups almond flour, 1/2 cup erythritol (powdered), 2 tbsp. psyllium husk powder, 1 1/2 tsp. baking powder, 1/4 tsp. nutmeg, 1/4 tsp. allspice, 1/8 tsp. ground clove, and 1/8 tsp. ground ginger.

4. By this point, the butter has started to smell nutty. Make sure that it's golden to a golden brown, then set aside (or in the fridge) to cool completely.

5. Once the butter is cool, mix the dry ingredients and set them aside for a moment. In a bowl, combine all wet ingredients. 2 large eggs, 1/2 cup heavy cream,

6. 1/3 cup browned butter, 1/4 tsp. (25 drops) liquid stevia, and 1/2 tsp. orange extract.

7. Using a hand mixer, beat together all of the wet ingredients until combined.

8. Sift 1/2 dry ingredients into the wet ingredients. You can use a colander to do this, or a proper sifter.

9. Use the hand mixer again to mix all of the dough. Repeat this process with the other half of the dry ingredients. Preheat your oven to 350F here.

10. Measure out all the dough into some silicone cupcake molds.

11. Bake for 20-25 minutes or until the top is golden brown around the edges.

12. Remove from the oven and set aside. Wait for about 5-10 minutes for this to cool.

13. Mix together cinnamon and erythritol (or xylitol). Melt 1/4 cup butter in a saucepan, and then turn the heat off. Dip each muffin into the butter (sides and bottom included) and then dip into cinnamon sugar

NUTRITIONAL VALUES210 Calories, 20.5g Fats, 5g Net Carbs, and 4g Protein.

Peanut pancakes

SERVES: 2

INGREDIENTS

- Roasted Peanut Filling
- 8 oz. Fresh Shelled Peanuts
- 1/2 tsp. Stevia
- Salt to taste
- Condensed Milk
- 1/4 cup Heavy Cream
- 2 drops Liquid Sucralose
- Apam Balik
- 1/2 cup Almond Flour
- 1/2 tsp. Bicarbonate Soda
- 1/2 tsp. Baking Powder
- 1/8 tsp. Salt
- 1/4 cup Almond Milk
- 1 large Egg
- 5 drops Liquid Sucralose
- 1/2 tsp. Vanilla Extract
- 1/4 tsp. Coconut Oil
- 1 tbsp. Unsalted Butter

DIRECTIONS

1. To prepare the peanut filling from scratch, roast 8 oz. Freshly Shelled Peanuts until brown.

2. Grind the peanuts, 1/2 tsp. Stevia and salt to taste with a pestle and mortar (or food processor). Set aside.

3. To prepare Condensed Milk, heat 1/4 cup Heavy Cream in a saucepan with 2 drops of Liquid Sucralose to a boil. Reduce heat and simmer. It should thicken up like condensed milk consistency. Let cool and set aside.

4. In a bowl, mix 1/2 cup Almond Flour, 1/2 tsp. Baking Soda, 1/2 tsp. Baking Powder and 1/8 tsp. Salt.

5. Add in 1/4 cup Almond Milk, 1 large Egg, 5 drops Liquid Sucralose, and 1/2 tsp. Coconut oil and mix well.

6. In a small pan on medium heat, melt and spread 1/8 tsp. (per pancake) Coconut Oil. Once hot, pour half of the mixture and cover the pan.

7. After 1 minute and the pancake is half-cooked, sprinkle half of the peanut filling. Spread half of the condensed milk onto one half of the pancake and butter onto the other half. Cover the pan once more for a few minutes.

8. Once the side is browned, remove the pancake and let it cool.

9. Repeat steps 6-9 for the other pancake. Once cooled, fold the pancake and slice to bite-sized pieces. Serve!

NUTRITIONAL VALUES

539 Calories, 50.7g Fats, 2g Net Carbs, and 11g Protein.

Low carb pancake sandwich

SERVES: 1

INGREDIENTS

- 0.75 oz. Pork Rinds
- 1 tbsp. Almond Flour
- 1 large Egg, beaten
- 1 tbsp. Heavy Cream
- 1/4 tsp. Vanilla Extract
- 2 tbsp. Maple Syrup
- The Filling
- 2 oz. Hot Sausage
- 1 slice Cheddar Cheese
- 1 large Egg

DIRECTIONS

1. Measure out 2 Oz. Sausage and set aside. You can use a silicone ring mold from Amazon to help with the whole process to keep everything the same size.

2. Grind pork rinds in a food processor until a powder is formed.

3. Heat a pan to medium-high heat on the stove. Add sausage in a ring mold and cook until medium-well temperature. Once cooked, set aside in some foil to rest.

4. While the sausage is cooking, mix pork rinds with all bun ingredients.

5. Put an egg ring mold inside the pan and fill 3/4 of the way with bun batter (this should be half of the batter).

6. Once the bun is browned on the bottom, remove the ring mold and flip to the other side. Cook until this side is also browned. Repeat the process with the other half of the batter to create another bun.

7. In the same pan, add an egg to the ring mold and lightly scramble. Cook completely until solidified.

8. Assemble with 1 bun on the bottom, 1 slice of cheese, hot egg, sausage, and the last bun on top. Then, serve!

NUTRITIONAL VALUES

657 Calories, 57g Fats, 7g Net Carbs, and 40g Protein.

Bacon avocado muffins

SERVES: 4

INGREDIENTS

- 5 Large Eggs
- 5 Slices Bacon
- 2 tbsp. Butter
- 1/2 cup Almond Flour
- 1/4 cup Flaxseed Meal
- 1 1/2 tbsp. Psyllium Husk Powder
- 2 medium Avocados
- 5 oz. Colby Jack Cheese
- 3 medium Spring Onions
- 1 tsp. Minced Garlic
- 1 tsp. Dried Cilantro
- 1 tsp. Dried Chives
- 1/4 tsp. Red Chili Flakes
- Salt and Pepper to Taste
- 1 1/2 cup Coconut Milk
- 1 1/2 tbsp. Lemon Juice
- 1 tsp. Baking Powder

DIRECTIONS

1. In a bowl, mix eggs, almond flour, flax, Psyllium, spices, coconut milk, and lemon juice. Leave to sit while you cook the bacon.

2. In a pan over medium-low heat, cook the bacon until crisp. Add the butter to the pan when it's almost done cooking.

3. Chop the spring onions and grate the cheese. Add the spring onions, cheese, and baking powder. Then, crumble the bacon and add all of the fat to the mixture.

4. Slice an avocado in half, remove the pit, and then cube the avocado while it's in the shell. Be careful of the sharp knife as you do this. Scoop out the avocado and fold into the mixture gently.

5. Preheat oven to 350F, measure out batter into a cupcake tray that's been sprayed or greased, and bake for 24-26 minutes. You should have leftover batter to make 4 more muffins, which you can do at the same time or afterward.

This makes a total of 16 **Avocado Bacon Muffins.**

NUTRITIONAL VALUES

163 Calories, 11g Fats, 5g Net Carbs, and 1g Protein.

LUNCH

Nasi lemak

SERVES: 2

INGREDIENTS
Fried Chicken

- 2 boneless Chicken Thighs
- 1/2 tsp. Curry Powder
- 1/4 tsp. Turmeric Powder
- 1/2 tsp. Lime Juice
- 1/8 tsp. Salt
- 1/2 tsp. Coconut Oil

Nasi Lemak

- 3 tbsp. Coconut Milk
- (from the can)
- 3 slices Ginger
- 1/2 small Shallot, sliced
- 1/4 tsp. Salt (or to taste)
- 7 oz. riced Cauliflower
- 4 slices Cucumber

Fried Egg

- 1 large Egg
- 1/2 tbsp. Unsalted Butter

DIRECTIONS

1. Prepare 7 oz. cauliflower rice (by ricing cauliflower) and squeeze water out.
2. Set aside.
3. Marinade 2 boneless Chicken Thighs with 1/2 tsp. Curry Powder, 1/4 tsp.
4. Turmeric Powder, 1/2 tsp. Lime Juice and 1/2 tsp. Salt. Set aside.
5. Prepare Sambal from this recipe on the website.
6. Fry the marinated chicken thighs until brown.
7. To prepare the rice, boil in a saucepan on medium heat: 3 tbsp. Coconut
8. Milk, 3 slices Ginger, 1/2 small Shallot, and 1/4 tsp. Salt (or to taste). It should take about a minute or less.
9. Once bubbling, add in the riced cauliflower and mix well.
10. Serve with 2 slices cucumber and a fried egg, along with 1 tbsp. Sambal and 1 piece Chicken Thigh.

NUTRITIONAL VALUES

507 Calories, 39g Fats, 9g Net Carbs, and 21g Protein.

Low carb sausage and pepper soup

SERVES: 6

INGREDIENTS

- 32 oz. Pork Sausage
- 1 tbsp. Olive Oil
- 10 oz. Raw Spinach
- 1 medium Green Bell Pepper
- 1 can Tomatoes w/ Jalapenos
- 4 cups Beef Stock
- 1 tsp. Onion Powder
- 1 tbsp. Chili powder
- 1 tbsp. Cumin
- 1 tsp. Garlic Powder
- 1 tsp. Italian Seasoning
- 3/4 tsp. Kosher Salt

DIRECTIONS

1. Heat olive oil in a large pot over medium heat. Once hot, add sausage to the pan.

2. Once the sausage is seared on one side, mix it to allow it to cook slightly.

3. As the sausage cooks, slice green pepper into pieces. I optionally add 1 jalapeno more because I prefer the spiciness of fresh jalapeno.

4. Add the peppers and stir everything together well. Season with salt and pepper.

5. Add the tomatoes and jalapenos from the can and stir once more.

6. Then, add the spinach on top of everything and place the lid on the pot.

7. Cook until spinach is wilted, about 6-7 minutes.

8. In the meantime, measure out all spices and grab your beef stock to have handy.

9. Once the spinach is wilted, mix it with the sausage. Then add the spices and mix again. Lastly, add the broth and mix once again.

10. Replace the lid and cook for 30 minutes covered, reducing heat to medium-low.

11. Remove the lid from the pan and let simmer for 15 minutes longer.

NUTRITIONAL VALUES

526 Calories, 43g Fats, 8g Net Carbs, and 28g Protein.

DINNER

Bbq chicken pizza

SERVES: 4

INGREDIENTS

Dairy-Free Pizza Crust

- 6 large Eggs
- 6 tbsp. Parmesan Cheese (omit for 2 tsp. coconut flour if going dairy free)
- 3 tbsp. Psyllium Husk Powder
- 1 1/2 tsp. Italian Seasoning Salt and Pepper to Taste

Toppings

- 4 oz. Cheddar Cheese
- 6 oz. Rotisserie Chicken, shredded
- 1 tbsp. Mayonnaise
- 4 tbsp. BBQ Sauce
- 4 tbsp. Rao's Tomato Sauce

DIRECTIONS

1. Pre-heat oven to 425F and shred cheese. Set aside.
2. Using an immersion blender, combine all ingredients for the crust until very well mixed. It should be rather thick.

3. Spread dough out on a Silpat using a silicone spatula. It's too sticky to use your hands for (I tried it and it was a mess). Silicone helps keep the dough from sticking on to everything. This will take you a few minutes to do, but your oven should be pre-heating in the meantime.

4. Once the crust is spread out evenly, place it in the oven and bake on the top rack for 10 minutes.

5. Once done in the oven, flip the pizza over. I tried flipping it with a flipper but ended up using my hands by holding 2 corners.

6. Top with your favorite toppings and then broil for an additional 3 minutes in the oven.

7. Slice and serve! Feel free to top with chives, spring onion, or other herbs/ vegetables that match the toppings.

NUTRITIONAL VALUES

357 Calories, 25g Fats, 9g Net Carbs, and 25g Protein.

Cheese stuffed bacon cheeseburger

SERVES: 2

INGREDIENTS

- 8 oz. Ground Beef
- 2 slices Bacon, pre-cooked
- 1 oz. Mozzarella Cheese
- 2 oz. Cheddar Cheese
- 1 tsp. Salt
- 1/2 tsp. Pepper
- 1 tsp. Cajun Seasoning
- 1 tbsp. Butter

DIRECTIONS

1. Season ground beef with all of the spices and mix lightly.
2. Prepare the cheese by cubing 1 oz. Mozzarella, and sliced 2 oz. of Cheddar.
3. Form rough patties with the ground beef and place mozzarella inside, enclosing the cheese with the beef.
4. Heat 1 tbsp. butter (per burger) in a pan, and wait until bubbling and hot.
5. Add burger to the pan.
6. Cover with a cloche and let cook for 2-3 minutes.

7. Flip the burger and place cheddar cheese on top. Place cloche over the top again and let cook until the desired temperature is reached, about 1-2 minutes more.

8. Chop bacon slice in half and place over the top of the burger. Enjoy!

NUTRITIONAL VALUES

614 Calories, 51g Fats, 5g Net Carbs, and 33g Protein

SNACKS

No bake chocolate peanut butter bombs

SERVES: 8

INGREDIENTS

- 1/2 CUP Coconut Oil
- 1/4 cup Cocoa Powder
- tbsp. PB Fit Powder
- tbsp. Shelled Hemp Seeds
- 2 tbsp. Heavy Cream
- 1 tsp. Vanilla Extract
- 28 drops Liquid Stevia
- 1/4 cup Unsweetened Shredded Coconut

DIRECTIONS

1   Mix all of the dry ingredients with the coconut oil. It may take a bit of work, but it will eventually turn into a paste.

2   Add heavy cream, vanilla, and liquid stevia. Mix again until everything is combined and slightly creamy.

3   Measure out unsweetened shredded coconut onto a plate.

4   Roll balls out using your hand and then roll in the unsweetened shredded coconut. Lay on to a baking tray covered in parchment paper. Set in the freezer for about 20 minutes.

NUTRITIONAL VALUES

208 Calories, 20g Fats, 0.8g Net Carbs, and 4g Protein.

Tortilla chips

SERVES: 6

INGREDIENTS

Tortilla Chips

- Flaxseed Tortillas
- Oil for Deep Frying, (~3 tbsp. Absorbed Oil)
- Salt and Pepper to Taste

Optional Toppings

- Diced Jalapeno
- Fresh Salsa
- Shredded Cheese
- Full-Fat Sour Cream

DIRECTIONS

1. Make the flaxseed tortillas using this recipe. I get 6 total tortillas when using a tortilla press.

2. Cut the tortillas into chip-sized slices. I got 6 out of each tortilla.

3. Heat the deep fryer. Once ready, lay out the pieces of tortilla in the basket.

4. You can fry 4-6 pieces at a time.

5. Fry for about 1-2 minutes, then flip. Continue to fry for another 1-2 minutes on the other side.

6. Remove from the fryer and place on paper towels to cool. Season with salt and pepper to taste.

7. Serve with toppings of choice!

This makes a total of 36 Tortilla Chips.

NUTRITIONAL VALUES

1g Fats, 0.04g Net Carbs (practically zero), and 0.9g Protein.

Jalapeno popper bombs

SERVES: 3

INGREDIENTS

- 3 oz. Cream Cheese
- 3 slices Bacon
- 1 medium Jalapeno Pepper
- 1/2 tsp. Dried Parsley
- 1/4 tsp. Onion Powder
- 1/4 tsp. Garlic Powder
- Salt and Pepper to Taste

DIRECTIONS

1. Fry 3 slices of bacon in a pan until crisp.
2. Remove bacon from the pan, but keep the remaining grease for later use.
3. Wait until bacon is cooled and crisp.
4. De-seed a jalapeno pepper, then dice into small pieces.
5. Combine cream cheese, jalapeno, and spices. Season with salt and pep-
6. per to taste.
7. Add the bacon fat in and mix until a solid mixture is formed.
8. Crumble bacon and set on a plate. Roll cream cheese mixture into balls using your hand, then roll the ball into the bacon.

NUTRITIONAL VALUES

207 Calories, 13g Fats, 5g Net Carb, and 8g Protein.

SIDE DISHES

Fried kale sprouts

SERVES: 1

INGREDIENTS

- 1/2 bag Kale Sprouts
- Oil for Deep Frying (~1 tbsp. Absorbed)
- 2 tbsp. Parmesan Cheese
- Salt and Pepper to Taste

DIRECTIONS

1 Heat the oil or lard in a deep fat fryer until it's hot. This is the package that I got from Trader Joe's, although I do know that they also sell Kale Sprouts in Whole Foods now.

2 Put kale sprouts in the fryer basket. Try to get the sprouts in a single layer.

3 Make sure that you close the deep fryer before submerging the basket into the oil. They have rather high water content and when water mixes with oil it can be quite violent – so splashing will occur.

4 Continue to fry the kale sprouts until they are browned on the edges of the bulb, and dark green on the leaves.

5 Remove from the basket and place on paper towels to drain any excess grease.

6 Add salt, pepper, and parmesan cheese. Enjoy!

Low carb broccoli and cheese fritters

INGREDIENTS

- 3/4 cup Almond Flour
- 1/4 cup + 3 tbsp. Flaxseed Meal
- oz. Fresh Broccoli
- oz. Mozzarella Cheese
- 2 large Eggs
- 2 tsp. Baking Powder
- Salt and Pepper to Taste

DIRECTIONS

1 Add broccoli to a food processor and pulse until the broccoli is broken down into small pieces. You want it to be well processed.

2 Mix the cheese, almond flour, flaxseed meal, and baking powder with the broccoli. If you want to add any extra seasonings (salt and pepper), do it at this point.

3   Add the 2 eggs and mix well until everything is incorporated.

4   Roll the batter into balls and then coat with flaxseed meal.

5   Continue doing this with all of the batters and set aside on paper towels.

6   Heat your deep fat fryer to 375F. I use this deep fat fryer. Once ready, lay broccoli and cheese fritters inside the basket, not overcrowding it.

7   Fry the fritters until golden brown, about 3-5 minutes. Once done, lay on paper towels to drain excess grease and season to your tastes.

8   Feel free to make a zesty dill and lemon mayonnaise for a dip. Enjoy

9   This makes 16 total Broccoli and Cheese Fritters.

NUTRITIONAL VALUES

Each fritter comes out to be 78 Calories, 8g Fats, 3g Net Carbs, and 6g Protein. With sauce, each fritter is 101 Calories, 3g Fats, 3g Net Carbs, and 6g Protein.

DESSERT

Low carb blackberry pudding

INGREDIENTS

- 1/4 cup Coconut Flour
- 1/4 tsp. Baking Powder
- large Egg Yolks
- 2 tbsp. Coconut Oil
- 2 tbsp. Butter
- 2 tbsp. Heavy Cream
- 2 tsp. Lemon Juice
- Zest 1 Lemon
- 1/4 cup Blackberries
- 2 tbsp. Erythritol
- drops Liquid Stevia

DIRECTIONS

1. Preheat oven to 350F. Then, separate the egg yolks from the whites and set them aside. You can save the egg whites to make different things like Low Carb Coconut Shrimp!

2. Measure out 1/4 cup Coconut Flour, and 1/4 tsp. Baking Powder. Set aside.

3. Measure out 2 tbsp. Coconut Oil and 2 tbsp. Butter. Set aside.

4. Beat the egg yolks until they're pale in color. Then, add 2 tbsp. erythritol and 10 drops of liquid stevia. Beat again until fully combined.

5   Add 2 tbsp. heavy cream, 2 tsp. lemon juice, and the zest of 1 lemon. Add the coconut and butter you had previously measured out and beat everything together until no lumps are found.

6   Sift the dry ingredients over the wet ingredients, and then mix well at a slow speed.

7   Measure out the batter into 2 ramekins and lightly smash the blackberries with your finger. Distribute the blackberries evenly in the batter by pushing them into the top of the batter.

8   Bake for 20-25 minutes at 350F. Once finished, let cool for 5 minutes or so.

9   Pour some heavy whipping cream over the top and eat! It's super delicious on its own too! You can share the ramekin with another, or eat it by yourself.

Blueberry lime July 4th cake

INGREDIENTS

- 1 cup Honeyville Almond Flour
- 2 tbsp. Coconut Flour
- 1 tsp. Baking Powder
- large Eggs, separated
- 2 tsp. Blueberry Extract
- 1/4 cup Fresh Blueberries
- 1/4 cup Cream Cheese
- 2 tbsp. Salted Butter
- 1/4 cup NOW Erythritol
- 1/4 tsp. Liquid Stevia
- Zest 1 Lime
- Juice 1 Lime

DIRECTIONS

1   Preheat oven to 325F. Separate the 5 eggs into 5 egg yolks in one container and 5 egg whites in the other.

2   Mix 1 cup Honeyville Almond Flour, 1 tsp. Baking Powder, and 2 tbsp. Coconut Flour.

3   Measure out 2 tbsp. Salted Butter and 1/4 cup Cream Cheese. Set aside for the time being.

4   Using a hand mixer, beat the egg yolks until they're pale in color.

5   Add 1/4 cup Erythritol, 1/4 tsp. Liquid Stevia, 2 tsp. Blueberry Extract, and the Butter and Cream Cheese to the egg yolks. Beat again until smooth.

6   Add Zest of 1 Lime and Juice of 1 Lime to the egg yolks (Save about 2 tsp. Lime Juice). Beat again until smooth.

7   Sift dry ingredients into the wet ingredients. You can just use a mesh colander to do this if you're lazy like me.

8   Mix the dry ingredients well into the wet ingredients.

9   Beat the egg whites with the 2 tsp. Lime Juice until stiff peaks form. Then, fold the egg whites into the mixture.

10   Pour the batter into your loaf or cake pans, then top with 1/4 cup Blueberries. You can get these awesome disposable cake pans from Target

11   Bake in the oven for 35-40 minutes or until you can cleanly remove a toothpick from the cake.

12   Let cool and serve!

Chocolate chunk cookies

INGREDIENTS

- 1 cup Almond Flour
- tbsp. Unflavored Whey Protein
- 2 tbsp. Coconut Flour
- 2 tbsp. Psyllium Husk Powder
- tbsp. Unsalted Butter
- 2 tsp. Quality Vanilla Extract
- 1/4 cup Erythritol
- drops Liquid Stevia
- 1/2 tsp. Baking Powder
- 1 large Egg
- bars Chocoperfection (or other 95%+ Cocoa Bar)

DIRECTIONS

1   Preheat the oven to 350F. Then, mix 1 cup Almond Flour, 3 tbsp. Un-flavored Whey Protein, 2 tbsp. Coconut Flour, 2 tbsp. Psyllium Husk Powder and 1/2 tsp. Baking Powder.

2   Using a hand mixer beat 8 tbsp. room temperature butter to a pale color. This should take about 1-2 minutes.

3   Add 1/4 cup Erythritol and 10 drops Liquid Stevia to the butter and beat again.

4   Add 1 large egg and 2 tsp. Quality Vanilla Extract to the beaten butter and beat again until well combined.

5   Sift dry ingredients over butter and mix again to combine fully. Make sure there are no lumps when you finish.

6   Chop the 5 bars of Chocoperfection (or other 95%+ Cocoa) and add to the dough. Mix well.

7   Roll the dough into a log. Make small markings over the top of the log to ensure consistent measurements of cookies.

8   Slice off each piece of dough and roll into a ball. Lay each ball onto a silpat that is on a baking sheet.

9   Using the bottom of a mason jar, lightly press the cookies flat into circles

10   Bake the cookies for 12-15 minutes or until a light golden brown color appears on the edges.

11   Let cool for 5-10 minutes before removing from the baking sheet.

12   Serve up with a nice glass of coconut or almond milk, and enjoy!

Pecan butter chia seed blondies

SERVES:

INGREDIENTS

- 2 1/4 cups Pecans, roasted
- 1/2 cup Chia Seeds
- 1/4 cup butter, melted
- 1/4 cup Erythritol, powdered
- tbsp. SF Torani Salted

Caramel

- drops Liquid Stevia
- large Eggs
- 1 tsp. Baking Powder
- 3 tbsp. Heavy Cream
- 1 pinch Salt

DIRECTIONS

1 Preheat oven to 350F. Measure out 2 1/4 cup pecans

2 Grind 1/2 cup whole chia seeds in a spice grinder until a meal forms.

3 Remove chia meal and place in a bowl. Next, grind 1/4 cup Erythritol in a spice grinder until powdered. Set in the same bowl as the chia meal.

4 Place 2/3 of roasted pecans in a food processor.

5 Process nuts, scraping sides down as needed until the smooth nut butter is formed.

6   Add 3 large eggs, 10 drops of liquid stevia, 3 tbsp. SF Salted Caramel Torani Syrup, and a pinch of salt to the chia mixture. Mix this well.

7   Add pecan butter to the batter and mix again.

8   Using a rolling pin, smash the rest of the roasted pecans into chunks inside of a plastic bag.

9   Add crushed pecans and 1/4 cup melted butter into the batter.

10 Mix batter well and then adds 3 tbsp. Heavy cream and 1 tsp. Baking Powder. Mix everything well.

11 Measure out the batter into a 9×9 tray and smooth out.

12 Bake for 20 minutes or until desired consistency.

13 Let cool for about 10 minutes. Slice off the edges of the brownie to create a uniform square. This is what I call "the bakers treat" – yep, you guessed it!

14 Snack on those bad boys while you get them ready to serve to everyone else. The so-called "best part" of the brownie is the edges, and that's why you deserve to have all of it.

15 Serve up and eat to your heart's (or rather macros) content!

This makes 16 total Pecan Butter Chia Seed Blondies

NUTRITIONAL VALUES PER BLONDIE

174 Calories, 11g Fats, 1g Net Carbs, and 9g Protein.

Cilantro infused avocado lime sorbet

SERVES: 4

INGREDIENTS

- 2 medium Hass Avocados
- 1/4 cup NOW Erythritol, Powdered
- 2 medium Limes, Juiced & Zested
- 1 cup Coconut Milk
- 1/4 tsp. Liquid Stevia
- 1/4 – 1/2 cup Cilantro, Chopped

DIRECTIONS

1   Slice avocados in half. Use the butt of a knife and drive it into the pits of the avocados. Slowly twist and pull the knife until put is removed.

2   Slice avocado half vertically through the flesh, making about 5 slices per half of an avocado. Use a spoon to carefully scoop out the pieces. Rest pieces on foil and squeeze the juice of 1/2 lime over the tops.

3   Store avocado in the freezer for at least 3 hours. Only start the next step 2 1/2 hours after you put the avocado in the freezer.

4   Using a spice grinder, powder 1/4 cup NOW Erythritol until a confectioner's sugar type of consistency is achieved.

5   In a pan, bring 1 cup Coconut Milk (from Carton) to a boil.

6   Zest the 2 limes you have while coconut milk is heating up.

7   Once the coconut milk is boiling, add lime zest and continue to let the milk reduce in volume.

8   Once you see that the coconut milk is starting to thicken, remove it and place it into a container. It should have reduced by about 25%.

9   Store the coconut milk mixture in the freezer and let it completely cool.

10   Chop 1/4 – 1/2 cup cilantro, depending on how much cilantro flavor you'd like.

11   Remove avocados from the freezer. They should be completely frozen along with the lime juice. The lime juice should have helped them not turn brown.

12   Add avocado, cilantro, and juice from 1 1/2 lime into the food processor. Pulse until a chunky consistency is achieved.

13   Pour coconut milk mixture over the avocados in the food processor. Add 1/4 tsp. Liquid Stevia to this

14   Pulse mixture together until desired consistency is reached. This takes about 2-3 minutes.

15   Return to freezer to freeze, or serve immediately!

NUTRITIONAL VALUES

180 Calories, 16g Fats, 5g Net Carbs, and 2g Protein.

Salted caramel glazed maple bacon cake pops

INGREDIENTS

- Maple Bacon Cake Pops
- Oz. Burgers' Smokehouse Country Bacon
- large Eggs, separated 1/4 cup Maple Syrup
- 1/2 tsp. Vanilla Extract 1/4 Cup NOW Erythritol 1/4 tsp. Liquid Stevia
- 1 cup Honeyville Almond Flour
- 2 tbsp. Psyllium Husk Powder
- 1 tsp. Baking Powder
- 2 tbsp. Butter
- 1/2 tsp. Cream of Tartar
- Salted Caramel Glaze 5 tbsp. Butter
- tbsp. Heavy Cream
- 2 1/2 tbsp. Torani Sugar-Free Salted Caramel

DIRECTIONS

1 Slice 6 Oz. Burgers' Smokehouse Country Bacon into small bite-size chunks.

2 Either freezing the bacon for 30 minutes prior, or using scissors normally helps with this process.

3 Heat a pan to medium-high heat and cook the bacon until crisp.

4 Once crisp, remove the bacon from the pan and allow to dry on paper towels. Save excess bacon grease to sauté vegetables or other meats in it.

5 Preheat oven to 325F. In 2 separate bowls, separate the egg yolks from the egg whites of 5 large eggs.

6 In the bowl with the egg yolks, add 1/4 cup maple syrup, 1/4 cup erythritol, 1/4 tsp. liquid stevia, and 1/2 tsp. vanilla extract.

7 Using a hand mixer, mix this for about 2 minutes. The egg yolks should become lighter in color.

8 Add 1 cup Honeyville almond flour, 2 tbsp. Psyllium husk powder, 2 tbsp. butter, and 1 tsp. baking powder.

9 Mix this again until a thick batter forms.

10 Wash off the whisks of the hand mixer in the sink to make sure all traces of fats are washed off of the whisks.

11 Add 1/2 tsp. cream of tartar to the egg whites.

12 Whisk the egg whites using a hand mixer until solid peaks form.

13 Add 2/3 crisped bacon into the cake pop batter.

14 Add about 1/3 of the egg whites into the batter and aggressively mix.

Caramel pots de crème

INGREDIENTS

- 1 1/2 cup Heavy Cream
- 1/4 cup NOW Erythritol (powdered)
- 1/4 tsp. Liquid Stevia
- 1/4 tsp. Salt
- large Egg Yolks
- tbsp. Water
- 1 tbsp. Maple Syrup (sub in 1 tsp. Maple Extract + 1/4 tsp. Xanthan Gum if you'd like)
- 1/2 tsp. Vanilla Extract
- 1 tsp. Maple Extract

DIRECTIONS

1   Preheat your oven to 300F. Start by separating the yolks of 4 eggs and setting them aside. You can save the whites to add to different cake recipes around the site.

2   Using a spice grinder (you can pick this one up cheap), powder 1/4 cup NOW erythritol. Be careful when you take the lid off because the powder will float into the air.

3   Mix the powdered erythritol with 6 tbsp. water in a small saucepan.

4   Mix 1 1/2 cups heavy cream, 1/4 tsp. liquid stevia, 1/4 tsp. salt, 1/2 tsp. vanilla extract, and 1 tsp. maple extract in a bigger saucepan.

5 Bright both of the mixtures to a rolling boil. Once the cream reaches a boil, stir vigorously and turn the heat down to low. Occasionally stir this as you work with the other mixture.

6 Once the water and erythritol have been boiling for a minute, add 1 tbsp. maple syrup. If you don't want to make the whole maple syrup recipe for 1 tbsp., you're welcome to sub in 1 tsp. Maple Extract + 1/4 tsp. Xanthan Gum if you'd like.

7 Whisk egg yolks well with a whisk until lighter in color.

8 Continue boiling the water and erythritol mixture until it has reduced some and watery syrup is formed.

9 Pour the water and erythritol mixture into the heavy cream and stir to combine.

10 Slowly pour 1/4 of the cream mixture into the egg yolks while mixing. You want to temper the egg yolks so make sure you add slowly and not too much at once.

11 Measure out the mixture between 4 or 6 ramekins depending on the size of the ramekin.

12 Fill baking sheet 2/3 of the way with water. Put your ramekins in the water and bake at 300F for 40 minutes.

13 Take out of the oven and let cool for 10-15 minutes. You cannot refrigerate them if you'd like them to be more of a light custard or pudding texture. You can eat them warm for a velvety soft and smooth texture.

Pine Nut Cookies

SERVES: 6

INGREDIENTS

- ¾ cup pine nuts
- 1 cup vegan margarine, softened
- ¾ cup sugar
- 1 teaspoon pure vanilla extract
- 2 cups all-purpose flour
- ½ teaspoon salt
- ¼ teaspoon baking powder

DIRECTIONS

1. Preheat the oven to 350°F. Finely grind ½ cup of the pine nuts and set aside.

2. In a large bowl, cream together the margarine and sugar until light and fluffy. Beat in the vanilla and set aside.

3. In a medium bowl, stir together the flour, salt, and baking powder. Add the flour mixture to the sugar-margarine mixture. Add the ground pine nuts to the dough, mixing well.

4. Drop the dough, 1 teaspoonful at a time, 2 inches apart, onto an ungreased baking sheet, pressing a few of the remaining ¼ cup pine nuts into the top of each cookie.

5. Bake until a light golden brown, 12 to 15 minutes. Cool on the baking sheet for 5 minutes before carefully transferring to a wire rack to cool completely. Store in an airtight container.

This makes about 3 dozen cookies

Chai Spice Cookies

INGREDIENTS

- 2 cups all-purpose flour
- 2 teaspoons baking powder
- 2 teaspoons ground cinnamon
- 1½ teaspoons ground cardamom
- 1 teaspoon ground ginger
- 1 teaspoon ground cloves
- 1 teaspoon ground fennel seed
- ½ teaspoon salt
- 1 cup vegan margarine
- 1 cup sugar
- 2 tablespoons plain or vanilla soy milk
- 2 tablespoons agave nectar
- 2 teaspoons pure vanilla extract

DIRECTIONS

1. Preheat the oven to 350°F.
2. In a medium bowl, combine the flour, baking powder, cinnamon, cardamom, ginger, cloves, fennel seed, and salt. Mix to combine well.
3. In a large bowl, beat together the margarine, sugar, soy milk, agave nectar, and vanilla until well blended. Add the flour mixture, stirring well to form a smooth, stiff dough.

4. Pinch off small pieces of dough and roll them between your hands into balls. Place the dough balls onto an ungreased baking sheet and use a metal spatula or a fork to flatten the cookies to about ¼

5. inch thick.

6. Bake until lightly browned at the edges, about 15 minutes. Cool on the baking sheet for 5 minutes before removing to a wire rack to cool completely. Store in an airtight container.

This makes about 2 dozen cookies

MEDITERRANEAN SEAFOOD

Louisiana Shrimp Esplanade

SERVES: 4

INGREDIENTS

- 24 large fresh shrimp
- ounces butter
- 1 tablespoon puréed garlic
- tablespoons Worcestershire sauce
- 1 teaspoon dried thyme
- 1 teaspoon dried rosemary
- 1/2 teaspoon dried oregano
- 1/2 teaspoon crushed red pepper
- 1 teaspoon cayenne pepper
- 1 teaspoon black pepper
- ounces beer
- cups cooked white rice
- 1/2 cup finely chopped scallions

DIRECTIONS

1 Wash shrimp and leave in the shell. Melt butter in a large frying pan and stir in the garlic, Worcestershire sauce, and seasonings.
2 Add shrimp and shake the pan to immerse the shrimp in butter, then sauté over medium–high heat for 4 to 5 minutes until they turn pink.

Next, pour in the beer and stir for a further minute, then remove from the heat.

3   Shell and devein the shrimp and arrange on a bed of rice. Pour the pan juices on top and garnish with chopped scallion.

4   Serve immediately.

Malibu Stir Fry Shrimp

SERVES: 4

INGREDIENTS

- 1 tablespoon peanut oil
- 1 tablespoon butter
- 1 tablespoon minced garlic
- 1 pound medium shrimp, shelled and deveined
- 1 cup sliced mushrooms
- 1 bunch scallions, sliced
- 1 red sweet pepper, seeded, cut in thin 2" strips
- 1 cup fresh or frozen peas
- 1 cup Malibu rum
- 1 cup heavy cream
- 1/4 cup chopped fresh basil or 1 tablespoon dried
- teaspoons ground chili paste or 2 tablespoons
- prepared chili sauce
- Juice of 1/2 lime
- Fresh ground black pepper
- 1/2 cup shredded coconut
- 1 pound fettuccine, cooked

DIRECTIONS

1   Heat oil and butter over high heat in a large pan.

2   Add garlic for 1 minute. Add shrimp, cook 2 minutes until pink. Add vegetables and fry for 2 minutes.

3   Add rum and simmer for 2 minutes. Add cream and simmer for 5 minutes.

4   Add remaining seasonings. Toss with coconut and cooked pasta.

Outa Sight Shrimp

SERVES: 4

INGREDIENTS

- pounds unpeeled, large fresh shrimp or 6-pound shrimp with heads on
- 1/2 cup butter
- 1/2 cup olive oil
- 1/4 cup chili sauce
- 1/4 cup Worcestershire sauce
- lemons, sliced
- garlic cloves, chopped
- tablespoons Creole seasoning
- tablespoons lemon juice
- 1 tablespoon chopped parsley
- 1 teaspoon paprika
- 1 teaspoon oregano
- 1 teaspoon ground red pepper
- 1/2 teaspoon hot sauce
- French bread

DIRECTIONS

1   Spread shrimp in a shallow, aluminum foil–lined broiler pan.

2   Combine butter and next 12 ingredients in a saucepan over low heat, stirring until butter melts, and pour over shrimp. Cover and chill for 2 hours, turning shrimp every 30 minutes.

3   Bake, uncovered, at 400 degrees F for 20 minutes; turn once.

4   Serve with bread, green salad, and corn on the cob for a complete meal.

Cool Shrimp Salad

SERVES: 4

INGREDIENTS

2 Lbs. Medium Shrimp

1 cup Miracle Whip

1/2 Cup Green Onions

1 Green Bell Pepper

1 Small Head of Lettuce

1 Medium Tomato

1/2 Cup Mozzarella Cheese

DIRECTIONS

1   Peel, devein, and boil shrimp. Chop lettuce, bell pepper, tomato, green onions, and shrimp, and mix in a bowl... Shred mozzarella cheese and add to salad.

2   Add miracle whip and mix well. Refrigerate for at least one hour and serve by itself or with your favorite seafood meal.

M-80 Rock Shrimp

SERVES: 4

INGREDIENTS

M-80 Sauce

- 1 tablespoon cornstarch

- 1 cup water

- 1 cup soy sauce

- 1 cup light brown sugar

- 1 tablespoon sambal chile paste

- cup freshly squeezed orange juice 1 serrano chile, finely chopped

- cloves garlic, finely chopped (about 1 tablespoon)

- One two-inch piece of fresh ginger scraped/peeled and finely chopped

Slaw

- head green cabbage, thinly sliced (about 1½ cups)

- head red cabbage, thinly sliced (about 1½ cups)
- medium carrot, thinly sliced into 2-inch pieces
- medium red pepper, thinly sliced
- medium red onion, thinly sliced
- 1 garlic clove, thinly sliced
- 1 Serrano chile, thinly sliced
- basil leaves, thinly sliced

Shrimp

- Vegetable oil
- 2-pound rock shrimp (or substitute 16-20 count shrimp cut into small cubes) 1 cup buttermilk
- 3 cup all-purpose flour
- Black and white sesame seeds
- 1 tablespoon green onions, thinly sliced
- Cilantro leaves

DIRECTIONS

1. Make the M-80 sauce: In a small bowl, whisk together the cornstarch and water. Set aside. In a small saucepan, whisk together the soy sauce, brown sugar, chile paste, orange juice, chile, garlic, and ginger, and bring the sauce to a boil.

2. Lower the heat and simmer for 15 minutes. Whisk in the cornstarch-water mixture and bring the sauce back up to a boil.

3. Make the slaw: In a medium bowl, toss together the green and red cabbage, carrot, red pepper, onion, garlic, chile, and basil. Set aside.

4. Make the shrimp: In a medium saucepan set over high heat, add enough oil to come halfway up the pot; heat until the oil reaches 350° (use a

thermometer to measure the temperature). Put the rock shrimp in a large bowl and pour the buttermilk over them.

5   Use a slotted spoon to remove the shrimp, drain off the excess buttermilk and, in a separate bowl, toss the shrimp with the flour. Fry the shrimp for 1 to 1½ Minutes.

Toast of the Town

SERVES: 4

INGREDIENTS

- Twelve 16-20 count shrimp, deveined and shells removed
- Salt and freshly ground black pepper
- avocados
- tablespoons lime juice (about 1 medium lime), divided
- tablespoons finely chopped cilantro
- teaspoons finely chopped jalapeño (about 1 medium jalapeño)
- 1 grapefruit
- 1 small baguette, sliced into ¼-inch slices Extra-virgin olive oil
- Salt and freshly ground black pepper ¼ cup pistachios, toasted and chopped

DIRECTIONS

1   Place the shrimp on a small plate and season with salt and pepper. Cut the avocados lengthwise around the pits and remove the pits. Cut the avocado flesh in a crosshatch pattern and use a spoon to scoop the avocado flesh into a medium bowl. Combine the avocado with 1½ tablespoons of the lime juice and the cilantro and jalapeño.

2   Use a knife to remove the skin and any pith from the grapefruit flesh and slice along the membranes to remove the segments. Set aside.

3   Brush the baguette slices with olive oil and season with salt and pepper. Place the baguette slices in the toaster and toast until golden brown.

4   In a medium skillet set over medium heat, heat 1½ tablespoons of olive oil and add the shrimp. Cook for one minute on one side, then flip and cook an additional 30 seconds on the other side. Transfer the shrimp to a bowl and toss with the remaining ½ tablespoon of lime juice.

5   To assemble: Spread 2 tablespoons of the avocado mixture on each baguette slice. Top with one or two pieces of shrimp and a segment of grapefruit. Sprinkle pistachios over the top and serve immediately.

Shrimp a la Plancha over Saffron Allioli Toasts

SERVES: 4

INGREDIENTS

- Allioli
- Large pinch saffron
- large egg yolks
- 1 garlic clove, finely chopped
- teaspoon kosher salt
- cup extra-virgin olive oil, preferably Spanish
- teaspoons lemon juice, plus more if needed
- **Shrimp**
- Four ½-inch-thick slices of country bread
- tablespoons good-quality extra-virgin olive oil, preferably Spanish
- 1½ pounds jumbo
- 16/20-count peel-on shrimp
- Kosher salt
- lemons halved
- garlic cloves, finely chopped
- 1 teaspoon freshly ground black pepper
- cup dry sherry
- tablespoons roughly chopped flat-leaf parsley

DIRECTIONS

1   Make the aioli: In a small skillet set over medium heat, toast the saffron until it is brittle, 15 to 30 seconds.

2   Turn it out onto a small plate and use the back of a spoon to crush it. To a medium bowl, add the saffron, egg yolks, garlic, and salt and vigorously whisk until well combined.

3   Begin adding the olive oil a few drops at a time, whisking thoroughly between additions, until the aioli begins to thicken, then drizzle the remaining oil into the mixture in a very slow and steady stream, whisking the aioli until it is thick and creamy.

4   Add the lemon juice, taste, and adjust with more lemon juice and salt as needed. Transfer to a small bowl, cover with plastic wrap, and refrigerate.

5   Make the toasts: Adjust an oven rack to the uppermost position and the broiler to high. Place the bread slices on a rimmed baking sheet and brush both sides of the bread with 1 tablespoon of the oil.

6   Toast the bread until golden-brown, about 45 seconds. Turn the bread over and toast the other side (watch the broiler closely, as broiler intensity varies), 30 to 45 seconds longer. Remove the bread from the oven and set each slice on a plate.

7   In a large bowl, place the shrimp. Use a paring knife to make a shallow slit down the curved back of the shrimp, removing the vein (if there is one) and leaving the shell intact. Heat a large, heavy-bottomed skillet over medium-high heat until nearly smoking, 1½ to 2 minutes.

8   Add the remaining 1 tablespoon of the oil and the shrimp. Sprinkle a good pinch of salt and the juice from half of a lemon over the shrimp and cook until the shrimp start to curl and the edges of the shell are browning 2 to 3 minutes.

9   Use tongs to turn the shrimp over, sprinkle with more salt and the juice from another lemon half and cook until the shrimp are bright pink, about 1 minute longer. Make a well in the center of the pan and stir in the garlic and black pepper; once the garlic is fragrant, after about 30 seconds, add the sherry, bring to a simmer and stir the garlic-sherry mixture into the shrimp.

10 Cook, stirring and scraping the brown bits from the bottom of the pan into the sauce. Turn off the heat and squeeze in the juice of another lemon half. Slice the remaining lemon half into wedges.

11 Spread the top of each slice of bread with a generous spoonful of the saffron aioli. Divide the shrimp among the plates and pour some sauce over each serving. Sprinkle with parsley and serve with lemon wedges.

Shrimp Curry with Mustard

SERVES: 4

INGREDIENTS

- 1 lb. shrimps
- 2 tbsp. oil
- 1 tsp. turmeric
- 2 tbsp. mustard powder
- 1 tsp. salt
- 8 green chilies

DIRECTIONS

1   Make a paste of mustard in an equal amount of water. Heat oil in a non-stick frying pan and fry the mustard paste and the shrimps for at least five minutes, and add 2 cups of lukewarm water.

2   Bring to a boil and add turmeric and salt and green chilies. Cook on medium-low heat for another twenty-five minutes.

Shrimp Curry

SERVES: 4

INGREDIENTS

- 1 lb. shrimps, peeled and deveined
- 1 onion, pureed
- 1 tsp. ginger paste
- 1 tsp. garlic paste
- 1 tomato, pureed
- 1 tsp. turmeric powder
- 1 tsp. chili powder
- 1 tsp. cumin powder
- 1 tsp. coriander powder
- 1 tsp. salt or to taste
- 1 tsp. lemon juice
- Cilantro/coriander leaves
- 1 tbsp. oil

DIRECTIONS

1. Heat oil in a non-stick frying pan and fry the onion, tomato, ginger, and garlic, together with cumin and coriander powders and cilantro/coriander leaves for five minutes on medium-low heat.
2. Add shrimp, turmeric and chili powders, and salt together with half a cup of lukewarm water and cook on medium-low heat for twenty-five

minutes. Keep the pan covered with a lid. Stir well to let the shrimps blend with the spices.

3   Season with lemon juice, garnish with cilantro/coriander before serving.

Note: Using pre-cooked, peeled, and deveined shrimp available in the grocery store to reduce preparation time.

Shrimp in Garlic Sauce

SERVES: 4

INGREDIENTS

- cloves garlic, roughly chopped
- 1 cup vegetable oil
- 1/4 cup (1/2 stick) unsalted butter
- 1 1/2 pounds fresh shrimp, peeled, deveined, and butterflied (leave tails intact)

DIRECTIONS

1   In a large skillet, sauté the garlic in medium−hot oil (about 300 degrees F) until light brown. Watch carefully so as not to burn.

2   After about 6 to 8 minutes, quickly whisk in the butter and remove it immediately from the fire. When all the butter has been added, the bits will become crisp.

3   Remove them with a slotted spoon and reserve the oil and butter for sautéing the shrimp.

4   In a large skillet, heat about 2 to 3 tablespoons of the reserved oil and then sauté the shrimp for about 5 minutes.

5   Turn over very briefly and then remove. Add more oil as necessary to sauté all the shrimp. Salt to taste.

6   Garnish with garlic bits and parsley. Serve with Mexican Rice.

7   Try brushing garlic oil over French bread, then sprinkling it with parsley and toasting it.

8   Serve this with the shrimp and accompany the dish with a lettuce and tomato salad.

Shrimp in Mustard Cream Sauce

SERVES: 4

INGREDIENTS

- 1 pound large shrimp
- tablespoons vegetable oil
- 1 shallot, minced
- tablespoons dry white wine
- 1/2 cup heavy cream or whipping cream
- 1 tablespoon Dijon mustard with seed
- Salt, to taste

DIRECTIONS

1 Shell and devein shrimp. In a 10-inch skillet over medium heat cook shallot in hot oil for 5 minutes, stirring often. Increase heat to medium-high. Add shrimp. Cook for 5 minutes or until shrimp turns pink, stirring often.

2 Remove shrimp to a bowl. Add wine to drippings in skillet. Cook over medium heat for 2 minutes. Add cream and mustard.

3 Cook for 2 minutes. Return shrimp to skillet. Stir until heated through. Salt to taste.

4 Serve over hot, cooked rice.

Gazpacho

SERVES: 4

INGREDIENTS

- 2 cloves garlic
- 1/2 red onion
- 5 Roma tomatoes
- 2 stalks celery
- 1 large cucumber
- 1 zucchini
- 1/4 cup extra-virgin olive oil
- 2 tablespoons red wine vinegar
- 2 tablespoons sugar Several dashes hot sauce Dash salt
- Dash black pepper
- 4 cups good-quality tomato juice
- 1 pound shrimp, peeled and deveined Avocado slices, for serving
- hard-boiled eggs, finely minced Fresh cilantro leaves, for serving Crusty bread, for serving

DIRECTIONS

1   Mince up the garlic, cut the onion into slices, and dice up the tomatoes, celery, cucumber, and zucchini. Throw all the garlic, all the onion, half of the remaining diced vegetables, and the oil into the bowl of a food processor or, if you like, a blender.

2   Splash in the vinegar and add the sugar, hot sauce, salt, and pepper. Finally pour in 2 cups of tomato juice and blend well. You'll have a tomato base with beautiful confetti of vegetables.

3   Pour the blended mixture into a large bowl and add in the other half of the diced vegetables. Stir it together. Then stir in the remaining 2 cups of tomato juice. Give it a taste and make sure the seasoning is right. Adjust as needed. Refrigerate for an hour if possible.

4   Grill or saute the shrimp until opaque. Set aside. Ladle the soup into bowls, add the grilled shrimp and garnish with avocado slices, egg, and cilantro leaves. Serve with crusty bread on the side.

Shrimp Linguine Alfredo

SERVES: 4

INGREDIENTS

- 1 (12 ounces) package linguine pasta
- 1/4 cup butter, melted
- tablespoons diced onion
- teaspoons minced garlic
- 40 small shrimp, peeled and deveined
- 1 cup half−and−half
- teaspoons ground black pepper
- tablespoons grated Parmesan cheese
- sprigs of fresh parsley
- slices lemon, for garnish

DIRECTIONS

1   Cook pasta in a large pot of boiling water until al dente; drain. Meanwhile, melt butter in a large saucepan.

2   Saute onion and garlic over medium heat until tender. Add shrimp; saute over high heat for 1 minute, stirring constantly.

3   Stir in half−and−half. Cook, stirring constantly, until sauce thickens. Place pasta in a serving dish, and cover with shrimp sauce.Sprinkle with black pepper and Parmesan cheese. Garnish with parsley and lemon slices.

Shrimp Marinara

SERVES: 4

INGREDIENTS

- 1 (16 oz.) can of tomatoes, cut up
- tbsp. minced parsley
- 1 clove garlic, minced
- 1/2 tsp. dried basil
- 1 tsp. salt
- 1/4 tsp. pepper
- 1 tsp. dried oregano
- 1 (6 oz.) can tomato paste
- 1/2 tsp. seasoned salt
- 1 lb. cooked shelled shrimp
- Grated Parmesan cheese
- Cooked spaghetti

DIRECTIONS

1 In a crockpot, combine tomatoes with parsley, garlic, basil, salt, pepper, oregano, tomato paste, and seasoned salt. Cover and cook on low for 6 to 7 hours.

2 Turn control to high, stir in shrimp, cover and cook on high for 10 to 15 minutes more. Serve over cooked spaghetti.

3 Top with Parmesan cheese.

MEDITERRANEAN PASTA

Parmesan Orzo

PREP TIME: 15 Minutes

COOKING TIME: 40 Minutes

SERVES 6

INGREDIENTS

- 1/2 C. butter, divided
- garlic powder to taste
- 8 pearl onions
- salt and pepper to taste
- 1 C. uncooked orzo pasta
- 1/2 C. grated Parmesan cheese
- 1/2 C. sliced fresh mushrooms
- 1/4 C. fresh parsley
- 1 C. water
- 1/2 C. white wine

DIRECTIONS

1. Stir fry your onions in half of the butter until it is browned then add in the rest of the butter, mushrooms, and the orzo.

2. Continue frying everything for 7 Minutes.

3. Now combine in the wine and the water and get everything boiling.

4. Once the mix is boiling, set the heat to low, and cook everything for 9 Minutes after adding in the pepper, salt and garlic powder.

5. Once the orzo is done top it with parsley and parmesan.

NUTRITIONAL VALUES

Calories 327 kcal, Fat 18.6 g, Carbohydrates 28.1g, Protein 8.6 g, Cholesterol 48 mg, Sodium 306 mg

Pasta Rustica

PREP TIME: 10 Minutes

COOKING TIME: 35 Minutes

SERVES 4

INGREDIENTS

- 1 lb. farfalle (bow tie) pasta
- 1 (8 oz) package mushrooms, sliced
- 1/3 C. olive oil
- 1 tbsp dried oregano
- 1 clove garlic, chopped
- 1 tbsp paprika
- 1/4 C. butter
- salt and pepper to taste
- 2 small zucchini, quartered and sliced
- 1 onion, chopped
- 1 tomato, chopped

DIRECTIONS

1. Boil your pasta for 10 minutes in water and salt. Remove excess liquid and set aside.
2. Fry your salt, pepper, garlic, paprika, zucchini, oregano, mushrooms, onion, and tomato, for 17 minutes in olive oil.

3. Mix the veggies and pasta.

NUTRITIONAL VALUES

Calories 717 kcal, Carbohydrates 92.8 g, Cholesterol 31 mg, Fat 32.9 g, Protein 18.1 g, Sodium 491 mg

Classical Alfredo

PREP TIME: 30 Minutes

COOKING TIME: 60 Minutes

SERVES 8

INGREDIENTS

- 6 skinless, boneless chicken breast halves
- 3/4 tsp ground white pepper
- cut into cubes
- 3 C. milk
- 6 tbsp butter, divided
- 1 C. half-and-half
- 4 cloves garlic, minced, divided
- 3/4 C. grated Parmesan cheese
- 1 tbsp Italian seasoning
- 8 oz. shredded Colb.y-Monterey Jack cheese
- 1 lb. fettuccini pasta

- 3 Roma (plum) tomatoes, diced
- 1 onion, diced
- 1/2 C. sour cream
- 1 (8 oz.) package sliced mushrooms
- 1/3 C. all-purpose flour
- 1 tbsp salt

DIRECTIONS

1   Stir your chicken after coating it with Italian seasoning in 2 tbsp of butter with 2 pieces of garlic.
2   Stir fry the meat until it is fully done then place everything to the side.
3   Now boil your pasta in water and salt for 9 Minutes then remove all the liquids.
4   At the same time stir fry your onions in 4 tbsp of butter along with the mushrooms and 2 more pieces of garlic.
5   Continue frying the mix until the onions are see-through then combine in your pepper, salt, and flour.
6   Stir and cook the mix for 4 Minutes. Then gradually add in your half and a half and the milk, while stirring until everything is smooth.
7   Combine in the Monterey and parmesan and let the mix cook until the cheese has melted then add the chicken, sour cream, and tomatoes.
8   Serve your pasta topped liberally with the chicken mix and sauce.

NUTRITIONAL VALUES

Calories 673 kcal, Fat 30.8 g, Carbohydrates 57g, Protein 43.3 g, Cholesterol 133 mg, Sodium 1386 mg

506 - Easy Italian Parmigiana

PREP TIME: 30 Minutes

COOKING TIME: 90 Minutes

SERVES 2

INGREDIENTS

- 1 egg, beaten
- 2 oz. shredded mozzarella cheese
- 2 oz. dry bread crumbs
- 1/4 C. grated Parmesan cheese
- 2 skinless, boneless chicken breast
- halves
- 3/4 (16 oz.) jar spaghetti sauce

DIRECTIONS

1. Coat a cookie sheet with oil then set your oven to 350 degrees before doing anything else.
2. Get a bowl and add in your eggs.
3. Get the 2nd bowl and add in your bread crumbs.
4. Coat your chicken first with the eggs then with the bread crumbs.
5. Lay your pieces of chicken on the cookie sheet and cook them in the oven for 45 minutes, until they are fully done.
6. Now add half of your pasta sauce to a casserole dish and lay in your chicken on top of the sauce.
7. Place the rest of the sauce on top of the chicken pieces. Then add a topping of parmesan and mozzarella over everything.

8. Cook the parmigiana in the oven for 25 Minutes.

9. Enjoy.

NUTRITIONAL VALUES

Calories 528 kcal, Fat 18.3 g, Carbohydrates 44.9g, Protein 43.5 g, Cholesterol 184 mg, Sodium 1309 mg

Diana's Favorite Pasta

PREP TIME: 20 Minutes

COOKING TIME: 55 Minutes

SERVES 4

INGREDIENTS

- 2 tbsps olive oil
- 1 (7 oz.) can oil-packed tuna, drained
- 1 anchovy fillet
- 1/4 C. diced fresh flat-leaf parsley
- 2 tbsps capers
- 1 (12 oz.) package spaghetti
- 3 cloves minced garlic
- 1 tbsp extra-virgin olive oil, or to taste
- 1/2 C. dry white wine
- 1/4 C. freshly grated Parmigiano-Reggiano
- 1/4 tsp dried oregano
- cheese, or to taste
- 1 pinch red pepper flakes, or to taste
- 1 tbsp diced fresh flat-leaf parsley, or to taste 3 C. crushed Italian (plum) tomatoes
- salt and ground black pepper to taste
- 1 pinch cayenne pepper, or to taste

DIRECTIONS

1. Stir fry your capers and anchovies in olive oil for 4 Minutes then combine in the garlic and continue frying the mix for 2 more minutes.
2. Now add pepper flakes, white wine, and orange.
3. Stir the mix and turn up the heat.
4. Let the mix cook for 5 minutes before adding the tomatoes and getting the mix to a gentle simmer.
5. Once the mix is simmering add-in: cayenne, black pepper, and salt.
6. Set the heat to low and let everything cook for 12 Minutes.
7. Now begin to boil your pasta in water and salt for 10 Minutes then remove all the liquids and leave the noodles in the pan.
8. Combine the simmering tomatoes with the noodles and place a lid on the pot. With a low level of heat warm everything for 4 Minutes.
9. When serving your pasta top it with some Parmigiano-Reggiano, parsley, and olive oil.

NUTRITIONAL VALUES

Calories 619 kcal, Fat 17.7 g, Carbohydrates 79.5g, Protein 31.2 g, Cholesterol 14 mg, Sodium 706 mg

VEGAN MAIN DISHES

Tamarind Chickpea Stew (Vegan)

SERVES: 4

INGREDIENTS

- 1 tablespoon olive oil
- 1 large onion, chopped
- 2 medium Yukon Gold potatoes, peeled and cut into ¼-inch dice
- 3 cups cooked chickpeas or 2 (15.5-ounce) cans chickpeas, drained and rinsed
- (28-ounce) can crushed tomatoes
- (4-ounce) can mild chopped green chiles, drained
- 2 tablespoons tamarind paste
- ¼ cup pure maple syrup
- 1 cup vegetable broth, homemade (see Light Vegetable Broth) or store-bought, or water
- 2 tablespoons chili powder
- teaspoon ground coriander
- ½ teaspoon ground cumin
- Salt and freshly ground black pepper
- 1 cup frozen baby peas, thawed

DIRECTIONS

1   In a large saucepan, heat the oil over medium heat.

2   Add the onion, cover, and cook until softened, about 5 minutes. Add the potatoes, chickpeas, tomatoes, and chiles and simmer, uncovered, for 5 minutes.

3   In a small bowl, combine the tamarind paste, maple syrup, and broth and blend until smooth. Stir the tamarind mixture into the vegetables, along with the chili powder, coriander, cumin, and salt and pepper to taste.

4   Bring to a boil, then reduce the heat to medium and simmer, covered, until the potatoes are tender, about 40 minutes.

5   Taste, adjusting seasonings if necessary, and stir in the peas. Simmer, uncovered, about 10 minutes longer. Serve immediately.

Pomegranate-Infused Lentil And Chickpea Stew (Vegan)

SERVES: 4

INGREDIENTS

- 1 cup brown lentils, picked over, rinsed, and drained
- 2 tablespoons olive oil
- ½ cup chopped green onions
- 2 teaspoons minced fresh ginger
- ¾ cup long-grain brown rice
- ½ cup dried apricots, quartered
- ¼ cup golden raisins
- ¼ teaspoon ground allspice
- ¼ teaspoon ground cumin
- ¼ teaspoon ground cayenne
- 1 teaspoon turmeric
- Salt and freshly ground black pepper
- ⅓ cup pomegranate molasses, homemade (recipe follows) or store-bought
- 2 cups water
- 1½ cups cooked or 1 (15.5-ounce) can chickpeas, drained and rinsed
- ¼ cup minced fresh cilantro or parsley

DIRECTIONS

1 Soak the lentils in a medium bowl of hot water for 45 minutes. Drain and set aside.

2 In a large saucepan, heat the oil over medium heat.

3 Add the green onions, ginger, soaked lentils, rice, apricots, raisins, allspice, cumin, cayenne, turmeric, and salt and pepper to taste. Cook, stirring, for 1 minute.

4 Add the pomegranate molasses and water and bring to a boil. Reduce heat to low. Cover and simmer until the lentils and rice are tender, about 40 minutes.

5 Stir in the chickpeas and cilantro. Simmer, uncovered, for 15 minutes, to heat through and allow the flavors to blend. Serve immediately.

Pomegranate Molasses (Vegan)

SERVES: 4

INGREDIENTS

- 2 cups pomegranate juice
- ⅓ cup sugar
- 2 tablespoons fresh lemon juice

DIRECTIONS

In a large saucepan, combine the pomegranate juice and sugar and cook over medium-high heat. Cook, stirring until the sugar dissolves. Reduce heat to low and simmer over medium-high heat until the sugar has dissolved, about 5 minutes.

Reduce heat just enough to maintain a simmer and cook until the juice thickens and reduces to less than a cup.

Stir in the lemon juice and pour into a container or jar with a tight-fitting lid. Let cool, uncovered, then store tightly covered in the refrigerator where it will keep for several days.

Autumn Medley Stew

SERVES: 6

INGREDIENTS

- 2 tablespoons olive oil
- 10 ounces seitan, homemade or store-bought, cut in 1-inch cubes
- Salt and freshly ground black pepper
- 1 large yellow onion, chopped
- 2 garlic cloves, minced
- 1 large russet potato, peeled and cut into ½-inch dice
- 1 medium parsnip, cut into ¼-inch dice chopped
- 1 small butternut squash, peeled, halved, seeded, and cut into ½-inch dice
- 1 small head savoy cabbage, chopped
- 1 (14.5-ounce) can diced tomatoes, drained
- 1½ cups cooked or 1 (15.5-ounce) can chickpeas, drained and rinsed
- 2 cups vegetable broth, homemade (see Light Vegetable Broth) or store-bought, or water
- ½ teaspoon dried marjoram
- ½ teaspoon dried thyme
- ½ cup crumbled angel hair pasta

DIRECTIONS

1   In a large skillet, heat 1 tablespoon of the oil over medium-high heat. Add the seitan and cook until browned on all sides, about 5 minutes. Season with salt and pepper to taste and set aside.

2   In a large saucepan, heat the remaining 1 tablespoon oil over medium heat. Add the onion and garlic. Cover and cook until softened, about 5 minutes. Add the potato, carrot, parsnip, and squash. Cover and cook until softened, about 10 minutes.

3   Stir in the cabbage, tomatoes, chickpeas, broth, wine, marjoram, thyme, and salt and pepper to taste. Bring to a boil, then reduce heat to low. Cover and cook, stirring occasionally, until the vegetables are tender, about 45 minutes. Add the cooked seitan and the pasta and simmer until the pasta is tender and the flavors are blended, about 10 minutes longer. Serve immediately.

Edamame Donburi

SERVES: 4

INGREDIENTS

- 1 cup fresh or frozen shelled edamame
- 1 tablespoon canola or grapeseed oil
- 1 medium yellow onion, minced
- shiitake mushroom caps, lightly rinsed, patted dry, and cut into ¼-inch strips
- 1 teaspoon grated fresh ginger
- green onions, minced
- 10 ounces firm tofu, drained and crumbled
- 2 tablespoons soy sauce
- 3 cups hot cooked white or brown rice
- 1 tablespoon toasted sesame oil
- 1 tablespoon toasted sesame seeds, for garnish

DIRECTIONS

1. In a small saucepan of boiling salted water, cook the edamame until tender, about 10 minutes. Drain and set aside.

2. In a large skillet, heat the canola oil over medium heat. Add the onion, cover, and cook until softened, about 5 minutes. Add the mushrooms and cook, uncovered, 5 minutes longer. Stir in the ginger and green onions. Add the tofu and soy sauce and cook until heated through, stirring to combine well for about 5 minutes. Stir in the cooked edamame and cook until heated for about 5 minutes.

3. Divide the hot rice among 4 bowls, top each with the edamame and tofu mixture, and drizzle on the sesame oil. Sprinkle with sesame seeds and serve immediately.

Yellow Dal with Spinach

SERVES: 4

INGREDIENTS

- 1¼ cups yellow split peas, picked over, rinsed, and drained
- 3½ cups water
- 1 teaspoon salt
- cups fresh baby spinach
- 2 ripe plum tomatoes, finely chopped
- ¼ cup chopped fresh cilantro
- 1 tablespoon canola or grapeseed oil
- 2 garlic cloves, minced
- 1 tablespoon finely chopped fresh ginger
- 1 serrano or another hot green chile, seeded and minced
- 1 teaspoon ground cumin
- ½ teaspoon ground coriander
- ½ teaspoon turmeric
- 2 teaspoons fresh lemon juice

DIRECTIONS

1. Soak the split peas in a medium bowl of hot water for 45 minutes. Drain and transfer to a large saucepan. Add the water and bring it to a boil. Add the salt, reduce heat to medium, and cook until split peas are tender and thickened about 40 minutes.

2. Add the spinach, tomatoes, and cilantro, stirring to wilt the spinach. Keep warm over very low heat.In a small skillet, heat the oil over medium heat. Add the garlic, ginger, and chile. Heat until fragrant, about 1 minute.

3. Remove from the heat and add the cumin, coriander, turmeric, and lemon juice, stirring to mix well. Add the mixture to the dal, stirring to combine. Serve immediately.

Three Lentil Dal

SERVES: 6

INGREDIENTS

- ½ cup green lentils, picked over, rinsed, and drained
- ½ cup brown lentils, picked over, rinsed, and drained
- 3 cups water
- Salt
- ½ cup red lentils, picked over, rinsed, and drained
- 2 tablespoons canola or grapeseed oil
- 1 medium yellow onion, minced
- 2 garlic cloves, minced
- 2 teaspoons grated fresh ginger
- 1 tablespoon hot or mild curry powder
- ½ teaspoon ground cumin
- ½ teaspoon ground coriander
- ¼ teaspoon ground cayenne
- 1 (14.5-ounce) can crushed tomatoes

DIRECTIONS

1. Soak the green lentils and brown lentils in separate medium bowls of hot water for 45 minutes. Drain the green lentils and place them in a large saucepan with the water. Bring to a boil. Reduce heat to low and simmer for 10 minutes.

2. Drain the brown lentils and add to the green lentils with salt to taste. Simmer, partially covered, for 20 minutes, stirring occasionally. Add the red lentils and simmer, uncovered, until the sauce thickens and the beans are very soft, 20 to 25 minutes longer.

3. In a large skillet, heat the oil over medium heat. Add the onion, cover, and cook until softened for about 10 minutes. Add the garlic and ginger and cook until fragrant, about 30 seconds.

4. Add the curry powder, cumin, coriander, cayenne, and tomatoes, stirring constantly for about 1 minute. Add the tomato mixture to the cooked lentils and stir to mix well. Cook another 10 minutes until the flavors are blended. Taste, adjusting seasonings if necessary. Serve immediately.

Black Bean And Bulgur Loaf

SERVES: 4

INGREDIENTS

- 1 tablespoon olive oil
- 1 medium yellow onion, minced
- 1 cup medium-grind bulgur
- 2 cups water
- Salt
- 4 cups cooked or 2 (15.5-ounce) cans black beans, drained, rinsed, and mashed
- ⅓ cup wheat gluten flour (vital wheat gluten)
- 2 tablespoons nutritional yeast
- 1½ teaspoons dried thyme
- 1½ teaspoons dried savory

- ½ teaspoon dried oregano
- ¼ teaspoon freshly ground black pepper

DIRECTIONS

1. In a large saucepan, heat the oil over medium heat.
2. Add the onion, cover, and cook until softened, 5 minutes. Add the bulgur and water and bring to a boil.
3. Salt the water, reduce heat to low, cover, and simmer until bulgur is tender and water is absorbed 15 to 20 minutes. If any water remains, drain well in a fine-mesh sieve, pressing any excess liquid from the bulgur.
4. Preheat the oven to 350°F. Lightly oil a 9-inch loaf pan and set it aside. Transfer the bulgur mixture to a large bowl.
5. Add the mashed beans to the bulgur. Stir in the oats, flour, yeast, thyme, savory, oregano, and salt and pepper to taste. Mix well until thoroughly combined.
6. Spoon the mixture into the prepared loaf pan, pressing with your hands to make a smooth loaf. Bake until firm, about 40 minutes. Remove from the oven and set aside to cool for 10 minutes before slicing.

Chickpea and Vegetable Loaf

SERVES: 4

INGREDIENTS

- 1 small white potato, peeled and shredded
- 1 medium carrot, shredded
- 1 small yellow onion, chopped
- 2 garlic cloves, minced
- 1½ cups cooked or 1 (15.5-ounce) can chickpeas, drained and rinsed
- 1 cup wheat gluten flour or chickpea flour, or more if needed
- 1 cup quick-cooking oats
- ½ cup dry unseasoned bread crumbs
- ¼ cup minced fresh parsley
- 1 tablespoon soy sauce
- 1 teaspoon dried savory
- ½ teaspoon dried sage
- 1 teaspoon salt
- ¼ teaspoon freshly ground black pepper

DIRECTIONS

1. Preheat the oven to 350°F. Lightly oil a 9-inch loaf pan and set them aside.
2. Squeeze the excess liquid from the shredded potato and place it in a food processor, along with the carrot, onion, and garlic.

117

3. Add the chickpeas and pulse to blend the ingredients while retaining some texture. Add the flour, oats, bread crumbs, parsley, soy sauce, savory, sage, salt, and black pepper. Pulse just until blended.

4. Scrape the mixture onto a lightly floured work surface. Use your hands to form the mixture into a loaf, adding more flour or oats if the mixture is too loose. Place the loaf in the prepared pan, smoothing the top. Bake until firm and golden, about 1 hour. Remove from oven and let stand for 10 minutes before slicing.

COOKING CONVERSION CHART

TEMPERATURE		WEIGHT	
FAHRENHEIT	CELSIUS	IMPERIAL	METRIC
100 °F	37 °C	1/2 oz	15 g
150 °F	65 °C	1 oz	29 g
200 °F	93 °C	2 oz	57 g
250 °F	121 °C	3 oz	85 g
300 °F	150 °C	4 oz	113 g
325 °F	160 °C	5 oz	141 g
350 °F	180 °C	6 oz	170 g
375 °F	190 °C	8 oz	227 g
400 °F	200 °C	10 oz	283 g
425 °F	220 °C	12 oz	340 g
450 °F	230 °C	13 oz	369 g
500 °F	260 °C	14 oz	397 g
525 °F	270 °C	15 oz	425 g
550 °F	288 °C	1 lb	453 g

MEASUREMENT			
CUP	ONCES	MILLILITERS	TABLESPOON
1/16 cup	1/2 oz	15 ml	1
1/8 cup	1 oz	30 ml	3
1/4 cup	2 oz	59 ml	4
1/3 cup	2.5 oz	79 ml	5.5
3/8 cup	3 oz	90 ml	6
1/2 cup	4 oz	118 ml	8
2/3 cup	5 oz	158 ml	11
3/4 cup	6 oz	177 ml	12
1 cup	8 oz	240 ml	16
2 cup	16 oz	480 ml	32
4 cup	32 oz	960 ml	64
5 cup	40 oz	1180 ml	80
6 cup	48 oz	1420 ml	96
8 cup	64 oz	1895 ml	128

Lightning Source UK Ltd.
Milton Keynes UK
UKHW020641030621
384863UK00011B/1168